ISBN: 978-1-7367131-0-5

Scripture taken from The Voice™. Copyright © 2008 by Ecclesia Bible Society. Used by permission. All rights reserved.

THE HOLY BIBLE, NEW INTERNATIONAL VERSION®, NIV® Copyright © 1973, 1978, 1984, 2011 by Biblica, Inc.® Used by permission. All rights reserved worldwide.

Scripture quotations marked NLT are taken from the Holy Bible, New Living Translation, copyright © 1996, 2004, 2015 by Tyndale House Foundation. Used by permission of Tyndale House Publishers, Inc., Carol Stream, Illinois 60188. All rights reserved.

Scripture quotations marked MSG are taken from THE MESSAGE, copyright © 1993, 2002, 2018 by Eugene H. Peterson. Used by permission of NavPress. All rights reserved. Represented by Tyndale House Publishers, Inc.

CELTIC WANDERINGS

A 40-Day Devotional

CINDY THOMSON

Cindy Thomson

EMERALD
PATH PRESS

In memory of all that was lost during the 2020 pandemic.
What was lost shall be found.

ALSO BY CINDY THOMSON

Finding Your Irish Roots: First Steps to Tracing Your Irish Line

Celtic Song: From the Traditions of Ireland, Scotland, England, and Wales

The Roots of Irish Wisdom: Learning from Ancient Voices

DAUGHTERS OF IRELAND SERIES

Brigid of Ireland

Pages of Ireland

Enya's Son

THE ELLIS ISLAND SERIES

Grace's Pictures

Annie's Stories

Sofia's Tune

Three Finger: The Mordecai Brown Story with Scott Brown

Visit www.CindysWriting.com

And sign up for my free newsletter

INTRODUCTION

I have long believed that the way to progress along the
Christian path is to look back at those who have traveled it
before us. I think most Christians would agree with that idea
because it's what we do by studying the Holy Scriptures. In
addition, I value learning from the stories of the ancient saints,
specifically those referred to as Celtic saints. With this in mind,
I've created this book that I hope will guide and encourage
you on your way.

Celtic wanderings did not consist of random stumbling
along dark paths. The pilgrimages the Celtic Christians took
might at first glance appear to be nothing more than random
jaunts without clear purpose. *Peregrinatio* is the Latin term for
a wanderer for Christ and is often used to describe these
ancient Celtic Christians who set sail on rudderless boats or
searched for hermitages in the wild. They weren't physically
headed for a destination such those who took pilgrimages to
the Christians sites of the day such as Rome, Italy, or Tours,
France. Spiritually-speaking they were in fact looking for
something in particular. The Promised Land, the place of our

resurrection as Christians. I invite you to join me on this spiritual quest within the pages of this book.

Many people make devotionals a part of their morning quiet time routine. While you may use these devotions anytime, consider changing things up by reading them in the evening or at bedtime instead. The Celtic people saw nighttime as a beginning rather than an ending as we tend to. The Celts celebrated their festivals after sunset when for them, a new day was beginning. An example of this is Halloween, or All Saints Eve, generally believed to have originated in Ireland and was observed during the dark half of the day. I have found evening devotionals to be calming and renewing after a busy a day. You might as well.

PART ONE

TRAVEL

Brothers, do not fear. God is our helper, sailor and helmsman, and he guides us. Ship all the oars and the rudder. Just leave the sail spread and God will do as he wishes with his servants and their ship.[1]

TRAVEL

Evening One

*Stand at the crossroads and look; ask for the ancient
paths, ask where the good way is, and walk in it, and you
will find rest for your souls. Jeremiah 6:16 NIV*

A good place to begin is with the concept of *peregrinatio*,
or pilgrimage, a practice the Celtic saints viewed as a high
priority. Edward Sellner in his classic work, **Wisdom of the
Celtic Saints**, says these ancient missionaries "… chose this
way of life out of deep devotion to Christ, but also perhaps
because of their genuine appreciation of God's mysterious
creation and their own desire to see the holy places and meet
people different than themselves."[2]

If they did that, shouldn't we? If, as Jeremiah the
ancient prophet said, we look for the ancient path, we will find
it involved some travel for these spiritual ancestors. Some
monks of long ago cast themselves out into the ocean on a
pilgrimage to find the place where one would live forever.
That place, of course, is with our Maker. They were not just

3

looking for Heaven but exploring their hearts as they forced themselves to face hardships, including as Sellner suggests, encountering other cultures.

Americans as a whole tend to travel less than Europeans do. There are many reasons for this, not the least of which is the fact that we live on a vast continent separated from many other cultures by great oceans. When given the chance, however, we must venture out a bit or risk becoming isolationists with only a narrow view of humankind. Book lovers have long known how to travel without going anywhere. The internet makes it possible to meet lots of people from all over the world while sitting on our couch. How we embark on this spiritual pilgrimage is not as significant as just deciding to do it. Reach out, take that ancient path of exploration and discovery, and listen along the way to what God is teaching you on your pilgrimage.

> CHALLENGE: Plan a pilgrimage, either an actual physical journey or through your thoughts and readings. Journal your reactions as you go and consider where God may be leading you.

> *Dear Father, show me where the ancient paths lie. Help me to venture out, travel physically when I'm able, but intellectually always, so that I may see others as you see them, including myself. Amen.*

TRAVEL

Evening Two

*By day the Lord went ahead of them in a pillar of cloud
to guide them on their way and by night in a pillar of fire
to give them light, so that they could travel by day or
night. Exodus 13:21 NIV*

Perhaps the most well-known story about travel in the
Bible is the Israelites' wandering in the desert. From that story
comes the image of God providing light: a pillar of cloud by
day and a pillar of fire by night to lead the way. Light in the
midst of darkness also had significance in the old Celtic
stories. As an infant, St. Brigid was said to emit light or be
surrounded by a light as she slept in her cradle, a luminous
indication of the Holy Spirit dwelling in her. St. Columcille
copied a stolen psalter at night with ease because his fingers
glowed like candles. Patrick defied a king's order by lighting a
paschal fire on a very dark night, drawing attention to his civil
disobedience. When the soldiers came for him, Patrick and his
followers appeared as a herd of deer and passed safely by
them. What these stories have in common is the illustration of
God providing even through the darkest night.

5

CHALLENGE: Sit in the dark and listen. Imagine the arms of Jesus protecting you. Picture yourself traveling forward without a candle, lantern, or flashlight, clinging to the hand of the One and feeling entirely safe and cared for. Remember this feeling the next time the dark threatens to overwhelm you. You are never alone.

Dear Father, let me feel your light even when I see nothing but darkness. You have provided for the saints of old. You will surely do the same for me today. Amen.

TRAVEL

Evening Three

Your word is a lamp for my feet, a light on my path.
Psalm 119:105 NIV

Keeping the fire burning in the hearth was extremely important in ancient times, not only for heat, but also for light. Imagine for a moment just how dark night would be without electricity or any power source. If you lived in the Middle Ages in the Celtic regions of Ireland, Scotland, Wales, or parts of Britain, you likely lived in a sparsely populated area. If your fire went out, chances were there was not another to draw from nearby. Outside your door lay a wild place where wolves roamed. A traveler without a torch faced the danger of falling into a bog even if he or she were successful in escaping predators. Now imagine the Celtic Christian trying to navigate his or her faith in the same vein, except swap the need of a torch for a lack of scripture. While it's true God can be seen in and his ways taught through nature and beside other believers (a centrally held belief of Celtic Christians), scripture was essential. Without it one would be in danger of falling prey to sin or straying far from God. The psalmist is referring to following God's laws and used this illustration because back then being without a lamp in the dark could be quite treacherous.

The ancient Celtic Christians lived by the Psalms. In the earliest days of St. Patrick and for a hundred or so years after, there were not many copies of the rest of the Bible. The Psalms were memorized and chanted in a song-like rhythm similar to what scholars believe was the psalmist's original intention. Psalm 119 contains multiple reminders of spiritually traveling by way of God's laws. I can picture the ancient monk or nun on a journey or imagine them simply moving from chore to chore while reciting this verse over and over, allowing the words to light the path.

CHALLENGE: Repeat this evening's verse several times. Then read Psalm 119 in its entirety. How has this influenced the way you think of scripture?

Dear Father, allow your words and your laws to light the depths of my heart. Help me to remember to meditate on these words as the day comes to a close. Amen.

TRAVEL

Evening Four

Now you've got my feet on the life path, all radiant from the shining of your face. Ever since you took my hand, I'm on the right way. Psalm 16:11 MSG

How do we know we're on the right path, the way of Jesus? As I've said earlier, asking is the way to find the ancient path. Our study of the ancient Celtic Christians is one way to "ask." The remaining question might be, will we find an answer? Matthew 7:7 (NLT) says, "Keep on asking, and you will receive what you ask for. Keep on seeking, and you will find. Keep on knocking, and the door will be opened to you." That's a promise. And God always keeps his promises.

In the late nineteenth century into the early twentieth, a man named Alexander Carmichael did a lot of asking. He and his family and colleagues traveled the Celtic regions of Scotland and the Outer Hebrides and recorded the ancient hymns, poetry, sayings, prayers, and incantations of the people. This vivid oral history had been in danger of being lost. I believe God's instruction to us to ask for the ancient paths serves both the purpose of ensuring we'll make our way

9

along the right road and that we will pass this information along.

The path is not always easily traveled. In fact, it's often not easy at all. Finding God and serving him through all our decisions is not something we alone are even able to achieve. How is it done? We can find the answer within Carmichael's collection, *Carmina Gadelica, Hymns and Incantations.*[3]

God be with thee in every pass,
Jesus be with thee on every hill,
Spirit be with thee on every stream,
Headland and ridge and lawn;
Each sea and land, each moor and meadow,
Each lying down, each rising up,
In the trough of the waves, on the crest of the billows,
Each step of the journey thou goest.[4]

CHALLENGE: Where will you look for God's path today? Make up your mind to find it no matter how difficult that proves to be.

Dear Father, I cannot find the path on my own. The way is dark. My feet stumble. I grow confused. Yet, with each step the way becomes clearer because you are holding my hand. Thank you for being the guide on my life's journey as I become more and more the person you created me to be. Amen.

PART TWO

GATHER

May the everlasting Father Himself take you
In His own generous clasp,
In His own generous arm.[5]

GATHER

Evening Five

*He tends his flock like a shepherd: He gathers the lambs
in his arms and carries them close to his heart; he gently
leads those that have young. Isaiah 40:11 NIV*

The word gather in this verse evokes a caring and
gentle image. A lamb requires tender care. It's comforting to
know that God sees us as tender lambs. The Celtic saints are
known for their fondness for animals. Brigid had a special red
cow. She fed a starving dog. She saved a wild boar from
hunters by offering it sanctuary. A white horse sensed
Columcille's impending death and laid his head on the saint's
chest and wept. Kevin once had a blackbird nest in his
outstretched hands as he was praying. He remained in that
position until the baby birds hatched in order not to disturb
them. Columcille's name means "Dove of the Church."
Cuthbert made friends with otters who would come warm his
feet as he prayed at night.

An example of how revered the wild animals were
comes from the margins of an eighth or perhaps ninth century
Irish text, translated by Kuno Meyer.[6]

13

A hedge of trees surrounds me.
A blackbird's lay sings to me.
Above my lined booklet
The trilling birds chant to me.
In a grey mantle from the top of bushes
The cuckoo sings.
Verily—may the Lord shield me!—
Well do I write under the greenwood.

As the Creator shielded the wild animals with shelter in the natural world, so he gathers us to himself.

CHALLENGE: The next time a squirrel on the road runs past your car or you hear a blue jay's squawk, give thanks to the God of all living things for his care and provision.

Dear Father, help me to feel gathered to you, protected and sheltered from harm. There is no safer stronghold. Thank you for caring for all of life. Amen.

GATHER

Evening Six

*"Whoever is not with me is against me, and whoever
does not gather with me scatters." The words of Jesus in
Matthew 12:30 NIV*

One of the largest Irish festivals in the world is held in
Milwaukee, Wisconsin, over a long summer weekend. I've
attended a couple of times to promote my books. When the
festival opens they celebrate with what they call "The
Gathering." At the close of the festival they hold "The
Scattering." These events are concerts featuring many of the
bands that performed over the weekend. I love this very Celtic
image and think it applies to Christians. We come together.
We gather for worship, mission work, and fellowship.

Another way to think of gathering comes from the Old
Testament where the death of a patriarch was frequently
spoken of as being "gathered to his people."

*Then Abraham breathed his last and died at a good old
age, an old man and full of years; and he was gathered to
his people. Genesis 25:8 NIV*

I love that image. It offers a sense of belonging rather than a sense of loss. Scattering, conversely, refers to going one's own way. Jesus called people to him. Those who refused the call were consequently scattered.

CHALLENGE: Think of a time when you felt scattered. How might circumstances have changed if instead you had returned to Jesus and found yourself gathered in his arms?

Dear Father, I want to be with you, not against you. Gather me in and help me to extend my reach and gather those around me so that no one is lost or alone. Amen.

GATHER

Evening Seven

For where two or three are gathered together in my name, there am I in the midst of them. Matthew 18:20 KJV

The ancient Celtic people gathered together for journeying, for worship, for work. While there were hermits sent out from their communities, rarely did anyone remain in that role for long. Christianity is about community, as God is in community in the Trinity: Father, Son, and Holy Spirit.

Jesus' example was followed as these Celts gathered. Brendan the Navigator took twelve followers with him on his great journey across the sea to find *Tir-na-n-Og* or Land of the Young. (If you're not familiar with this story, learn more in my book, *The Roots of Irish Wisdom: Learning From Ancient Voices*. Many believe St. Brendan was the first European to discover America!) Twelve plus the abbot mirrored the example of Jesus and his disciples. Likewise, Columcille took twelve brothers along on his many journeys, including his banishment to Iona.

17

Matthew tells us, however, only two or three gathered are needed for God to acknowledge the assembly. The Celtic Christians observed this through the concept of *anamchara*, or soul friend. The late John O'Donohue, in his book, *Anam Cara: A Book of Celtic Wisdom*, explains that anam is Gaelic for soul and cara (or chara) means friend. I've read elsewhere that the correct spelling is anamchara when the two words are put together. O'Donohue emphasized the meaning, thus he spells it differently in his book. For the ancient Celtic Christians, a confessor was referred to as anamchara, someone with whom to share one's innermost thoughts and feelings and with whom to confess sins. This type of friendship brought an acknowledgement and belonging that could not be dissolved even by distance. O'Donohue says, "Where you are understood, you are at home."[7] How lovely is that? Surely a basic human desire is to be understood. This is the true nature of God, someone who loves us so completely, who never leaves us, who understands. One who embraces us in true friendship and welcomes us home.

CHALLENGE: Consider your relationships. Is there anyone you share yourself so completely with because when you gather together, God is there too? If not, challenge yourself to seek out two or three you can meet with and sense God's presence.

Dear Father, thank you for the gift of friendship and love. Thank you for always being there when I gather together with others and for understanding my hopes and fears. Help me to extend that kind of love and acceptance to others. Amen.

GATHER

Evening Eight

And let us not neglect our meeting together, as some people do, but encourage one another, especially now that the day of his return is drawing near. Hebrews 10:25 NLT

The Celtic Christians did not believe, or perhaps even imagine, that the faith could be practiced alone. They built communities that grew so vast and influential that Europeans came to Ireland to be educated. While the Celts underwent pilgrimages and some took turns living in hermitages, these were temporary pursuits with the purpose of holding the community up in prayer. They were not selfish quests nor punishments for sins. When the time away came to an end, these religious people met up again because they did not "neglect meeting together." Have you ever tried to encourage yourself? I'd venture to say it's not possible. We need each other. This was the way of the Celtic Christians. The need for encouragement has not gone away over the centuries, despite a plethora of entertainment options for distraction, including that black hole called the internet. If the coronavirus pandemic taught us nothing else, it revealed how much we need to gather together. Time alone is golden, but too much is, well, too much.

> CHALLENGE: If you've been away from the fellowship of other believers, or perhaps one in particular you are thinking of right now, make it a point to reconnect. Pick up the phone, write an email, send a letter, make a coffee date. Do not neglect that gathering because one day you will appreciate the encouragement you received from it and will be glad you gave as well.

> *Dear Father, thank you for the opportunities that exist to connect with those who know you. Remind me not to neglect gathering together with them. Amen.*

PART THREE

LISTEN

Let us do the will of God,
Let us merit the life of the saints,
Let us hear the voice of the angels,
And see the light of heaven.[8]

LISTEN

Evening Nine

"Since they refused to listen when I called to them, I would not listen when they called to me," says the Lord of Heaven's Armies. Zechariah 7:13 NLT

While our Celtic Christian ancestors prayed and pleaded, they also spent a lot of time listening. Listening is an underappreciated virtue in our day but is just as important as ever. This verse, however, is about something a little different. In this context it refers to obedience. The Israelites may have heard God's voice clearly, they just weren't obeying. How many times a day do parents admonish their children to listen? God wants the same thing. He wants his children to listen. The consequence of not obeying was severe. God would no longer hear their petitions. He would no longer send his army of angels to fight on their behalf. No believer wants that.

I wrote a section on Celtic prayer in my book, *The Roots of Irish Wisdom*. In it I talk about how the Celtic Christians were focused on the type of prayer that God would hear. The importance of an anamchara/confessor is stressed. "Praying

25

for someone else was just as important as having someone hear your confession and pray for you. The belief was that interceding in prayer for others prompted God to open his ears and grant a blessing. A desire for God to hear one's prayers was just as important to the ancient Irish Christians as it was to the psalmist when he said, 'I call to you, O God, for you will answer me; give ear to me and hear my prayer.'" (Psalm 17:6).[9]

Like the interweaving of a Celtic knot, our need to have God hear us is connected with his desire to have us hear him, and in turn be attuned to the needs of others, which he instructs us to do.

Therefore confess your sins to each other and pray for each other so that you may be healed. The prayer of a righteous person is powerful and effective. James 5:16 NIV

CHALLENGE: Before you begin to pray, consider what is happening in the lives of those around you. Bring their petitions before God and then listen for what God is already doing in the world before you speak your own prayers.

Dear Father, train my ears to notice your work in the natural world and your hand on the lives of all your children. Give me a heart to help before asking for help for myself. Help me to quiet the voices in my own mind and just sit with you awhile. Amen.

LISTEN

Evening Ten

Come here and listen, O nations of the earth. Let the world and everything in it hear my words. Isaiah 34:1 NLT

The pre-Christian Celts viewed certain places in the natural landscape as sacred. Stones, trees, hilltops, even a gentle rise in the landscape could be viewed as locations where the supernatural was at play. Newgrange, a Stone Age passage tomb located in the Boyne Valley in County Meath, Ireland, is a 5,200-year-old manmade structure where during the winter solstice rays of sunrise pass through a narrow chamber. The use of a natural occurrence not yet understood scientifically was nonetheless seen as spiritually significant by the ancients. Author Tracy Balzer says, "The earliest pagan Celts were profoundly aware of the spiritual world. Even before they came to know the one true God of the universe, they had an understanding of the unseen world, and perceived the reality of the spiritual world at every turn."[10] This didn't go away just because Patrick and other early

Christians began to convert the people. Instead, the belief in sacred places was passed on. There are many such places preserved today. One for me is Saul, near Downpatrick in County Down, Northern Ireland. Although the church there was built in modern times, the area holds a kind of quiet reverence. It's believed that Patrick built his first church near there, but Saul was a sacred place to the druids before that. Walking on the grounds and inside the stone church, I felt as though the prayers of those I could not see surrounded me. Prayers of petition, prayers of sorrow, and even joyful prayers. The grass, the yews, the flagstones—everything around me seemed to teem with prayers I could feel. Everything in the world, as Isaiah says. And this sense came to me through listening and keeping my mind still as I explored the site.

In the ancient Christian world there existed what was called thin places. These places can still be found today anywhere in the world. These are spots where it is believed that the veil between earth and heaven is so thin one can "see" them both. The realms seem to touch in these sacred spaces. I once asked J. Philip Newell, author of *Listening For the Heartbeat of God,* and many other books on Celtic spirituality, why certain spots were considered thin places. He told me he thought the wilderness was often where people listened and observed best. Because of that they could more easily sense God at work. Truly, you can find a thin place anywhere you prepare yourself to be in an attitude of listening. Certainly, those spaces where the power and wonder of God are clearly evident, like Iona or Lindisfarne for example, are thin places. But so also can a desert in New Mexico or a meadow in Kansas become thinly veiled if the seeker is listening for God. Newell also thought thin places can be found in metro areas. The challenge comes in finding quiet. Perhaps that's why in Matthew are we advised to, "… go into your room, close the door and pray to your Father, who is unseen." (Matthew 6:6 NIV).

CHALLENGE: Find one thin place you can visit often. Give yourself some time and quiet and just listen. Bring a journal and write down your observations.

Dear Father, lead me to a thin place. Give me ears to listen. Amen.

LISTEN

Evening Eleven

And the Lord came and called as before, "Samuel! Samuel!" And Samuel replied, "Speak, your servant is listening." 1 Samuel 3:10 NLT

I grew up on Bible stories, at least the ones I heard in Sunday school. The story of God calling to Samuel was one of them. Samuel kept hearing his name called in the middle of the night. He thought the old man he worked for was calling for him. Every time Samuel would go to him, Eli told him he hadn't called and he should go back to bed. But it kept happening. This chapter opens by telling us in those days messages and visions from God were rare, so we can't blame Eli for taking so long to figure this out. Finally, he told Samuel what to do. Tell God you are listening.

I remember when I was young thinking that if I heard my name called in the middle of the night, I had better do as Samuel did. I wouldn't want God to think I wasn't willing and ready to hear him. I never entertained the idea that it might never happen to me. I was sure it might at any time. Then I grew up and lost a bit of that childlike faith. I think growing up causes us to have to work hard at listening for God's voice. We've convinced ourselves the voice won't come. We've told ourselves God only speaks through burning bushes or lightening or signs written in the clouds. God may speak that way, but more often he does not. That's why finding a time for contemplation and quiet prayer is so important. It's a time when we can finally say, "Speak, your servant is listening."

In the 1977 movie, *Oh, God!* starring John Denver as Jerry Landers, God, in the form of George Burns, appears to a grocery store manager who has a difficult time convincing the established clergy that he has heard God speaking to him. It's a humorous story that hints at the truth: God speaks to all, even the least of us, and sometimes even to non-believers, as Denver's character was at first. It took some convincing, but Jerry the grocery store manager does listen and he brings God's message onto the stage of a television evangelist. Jerry became a willing servant, much like the biblical Samuel. In the end, Jerry believes he's failed, but God tells him he's only been planting seeds and time will tell where they take root. God is preparing to take a trip and doesn't plan on coming back any time soon. Jerry asks if they can just talk again sometime. God says, "I'll tell you what. You talk, I'll listen." That's probably the best theology in the film. Jerry proved himself to be a good listener and servant and so God will listen if Jerry wants to talk.

> CHALLENGE: Think about the best relationships in your life. What makes them work so well? How might you apply those things to your relationship with the Creator?

> *Dear Father, I want to be like Samuel, a ready and willing servant whenever you speak to me. Thank you for listening to me, for caring for me, and for speaking to me. Amen.*

LISTEN

Evening Twelve

*You, Lord, hear the desire of the afflicted; you encourage
them, and you listen to their cry ...*
Psalm 10:17 NIV

In Esther De Waal's book, *Every Earthly Blessing:
Rediscovering the Celtic Tradition*, she talks about healing plants
and the belief that because Christ came to earth and we have
stories of many of his acts of healing, the Celtic Christians
alleged that he touched certain plants while he was on earth
and gave them healing capabilities. In referencing Alexander
Carmichael's work, she says the people of the Outer Hebrides
told stories as though Jesus and his mother still walked among
them. "If a woman healed a blind eye she might remind
herself of the story of the time that Mary had restored the sight
of the salmon. Again she would speak of it almost as if the
scene, though in the Holy Land, had actually taken place in
the familiar countryside."[11]

These stories brought great comfort and
encouragement. Christ once walked among the common

people so he can still be present right now where I am. He heard the cries of the afflicted then, he hears them now. He listened and healed then, and he does so now. The Celtic Christians had a keen sense of how close God is. Their religion was personal and intimate.

CHALLENGE: How do you view God? Far away in heaven or as close as your next breath? Spend a moment imagining Jesus sitting with you and listening to your physical complaints. What will you tell him?

Dear Father, help me right now in this moment feel your presence, your comfort, your encouragement. Touch and heal all the places where I feel pain. Thank you for hearing me. Amen.

PART FOUR

REMEMBER

God, you make us glad
With the weekly remembrance
Of the glorious resurrection of your Son.[12]

REMEMBER

Evening Thirteen

They refused to listen and failed to remember the miracles you performed among them. They became stiff-necked and in their rebellion appointed a leader in order to return to their slavery. Nehemiah 9:17 NIV

The above scripture was spoken by the Israelites confessing their sins to God. The chapter explains what they did in order. They fasted, confessed their sins and those of their ancestors, they read the Book of Law, they worshiped, they praised God, they listed the history of what God had done for them in the past, and then comes verse 17. They knew that their ancestors had failed to remember, and they understood what they became as a result of that failure. They had gone astray mainly because they'd forgotten all these things.

The ancient Celtic monks also wanted to remember what God had done. They valued education and the ability to read scriptures for themselves, but because books were rare, they spent much of their lives memorizing and copying as much as they could. They also fasted and confessed their sins, read as much as possible, praised God the Creator of all things, remembered to count their blessings, and remembered the stories of old.

This was the purpose of the high crosses that depict biblical stories. The majority of scriptural crosses are believed to have been erected in the eighth or ninth century. Today they appear gray, washed by centuries of wind, rain, and frost. However, the crosses may once have been colorfully painted, much like the well-known illuminated manuscript *The Book of Kells*. The Cross of the Scriptures at Clonmacnoise, County Offaly, was carved and erected by Abbot Colman in honor of King Flann, who died in 914 CE. We know this from the inscription on the cross itself. Flann was high king at Tara during the time of the erection of the Scripture Cross. The original cross is now inside the visitors' center. A replica stands in its place outside. I have seen this high cross and have marveled at the engravings, imagining crowds of people standing around learning the stories and then contemplating what they saw engraved on these lofty monuments as they returned to their chores. A visual aid helps recall, as any elementary teacher can tell you. The Israelites sought to remember the story of the parting of the Red Sea that allowed

them to pass safely through while their pursuers were
drowned. The ancient Irish remembered that very story
through carvings of the scene on the Ruined Cross at Kells.

> CHALLENGE: Find a story in the Bible that is either new to
> you or not very well remembered. Contemplate the story and
> remember what God has done.

> *Dear Father, help me to use whatever aids are available*
> *to me so that I will never forget the miracles, wonders,*
> *and blessings you have bestowed on your people*
> *throughout the ages. Amen.*

REMEMBER

Evening Fourteen

But God remembered Noah and all the wild animals and the livestock that were with him in the ark, and he sent a wind over the earth, and the waters receded. Genesis 8:1 NIV

The story of the flood is well represented on Ireland's high crosses. This story beautifully illustrates God's restorative power. He did not forget Noah and the animals who had survived a colossal worldwide disaster. God saved a small remnant of human existence. He remembered. He sent the wind to dry up the waters for Noah and his family. God always makes a way.

It was this belief that prompted St. Brendan and his followers to make their journey. The boats in those days were rudderless crafts of animal skin waterproofed with tanned oak bark. In the 1970s a man named Tim Severin recreated Brendan's sixth-century journey as authentically as possible, sailing from Ireland to North America. Severin wanted to prove that the old tale was feasible. He built the kind of boat Brendan would have used. That replica is now on display at the Craggaunowen, a living history museum in County Clare, Ireland, where visitors can see for themselves how perilous the journey must have been in that type of craft. Like Noah, Brendan trusted that God would not forget him, and he did not.

> CHALLENGE: Are you aware of your comfort zones, the places you believe God wants you to step out of and trust him? Decide to take one step today.

Dear Father, give me the faith to leave old ways and
break fresh ground with You.
Christ of the mysteries, I trust You to be stronger than
each storm within me.
I will trust in the darkness and know that my times, even
now, are in Your hand.
Tune my spirit to the music of heaven, and somehow,
make my obedience count for You.
Amen. (Prayer attributed to St. Brendan)

REMEMBER

Evening Fifteen

*Remember the Sabbath day by keeping it holy. Exodus
20:8 NIV*

This commandment tells us the Sabbath is a time of rest
and a time to remember to keep it holy, which means
dedicating the Sabbath to God. Easy to forget, especially in
modern society where church attendance has been falling off a
cliff, at least in the United States. How did the ancient Celtic
Christians keep the Sabbath holy? For the monks in religious
communities that wasn't a problem. They already followed a
strict discipline daily.

"He should be constant in prayer, never forgetting his
canonical hours. Let him give his mind to his prayer with
humility and with great peace."

~From the Rule of St. Ailbe, a sixth-century Irish monk.

"Do not profane the Sabbath of the Son of God, but
conduct your business at the proper time. On Sundays
meditate on the scriptures, read them aloud and make copies
of them."

~From the Rule of Ciarán, a sixth-century Irish monk.[13]

Neither was it difficult for others who looked forward to a day of rest from their labors. In 2001 the *Irish Times* ran an editorial by someone referred to as F.MacE. In it he complained about the cost to our health and wellbeing when the Sabbath is ignored. He wished to return to what Sunday used to mean in Ireland: "A trip to church, a family lunch, a call in on Granny, watching a football match, going for a pint. Work tomorrow was a universe away. One day every week should be very different from the other six."[14]

I agree. Rest and postponing all non-essential work for one day is healthy and restorative. So is using that time for spiritual contemplation.

> CHALLENGE: Seek to make one change on whatever day you can to observe Sabbath. Make note of the benefits you observe in your health and emotional outlook.

Dear Father,
God of holy rest,
on the seventh day you paused,
laying down the work of creation
and entered into sacred stillness.
Kindle in me the strength to say no
to a world of perpetual busyness.
Sustain in me the desire to simply be.
Let my life be a loving witness to
a world of restoration and renewal,
joy and laughter.
~Christine Balters Paintner, used with permission[15]
Amen.

REMEMBER

Evening Sixteen

Fix these words of mine in your hearts and minds; tie them as symbols on your hands and bind them on your foreheads. Teach them to your children, talking about them when you sit at home and when you walk along the road, when you lie down and when you get up. Write them on the doorframes of your houses and on your gates, so that your days and the days of your children may be many in the land the LORD swore to give your ancestors, as many as the days that the heavens are above the earth. Deuteronomy 11:18-21 NIV

This is one of my favorite passages on the topic of remembering God's commandments. Moses gave no less than eight suggestions to help the people remember. The Jewish tradition involves some literal interpretations such as the *mezuzah*, which means doorpost, a piece of parchment with some verses from Deuteronomy written on them and affixed to the door frame at the entrance of the house.

Symbols can serve as memory aides. Many churches are filled with Christian symbolism. The cross is the most recognizable. The early Celtic Christians also used symbols and designs, and many can be seen still on high crosses, other stones, and manuscripts. Some predate Christianity and were adopted and given Christian meaning. This doesn't bother me because the purpose is to remember, and if a symbol helps you to remember a Christian precept that is what matters most. There are a few Celtic symbols that perhaps aren't as well known today. Below are a few along with the meaning Christians have attached to them.

St. Brigid's Cross: This wheel-shaped cross is woven from rushes on the eve of her feast day, February 1. The legend is that she wove the cross while tending to a dying pagan. She explained Jesus' sacrifice as she worked, and the man was saved before he died.

Shamrock: This symbol reminds most people of Ireland and perhaps St. Patrick, but it can mean much more. The legend is that St. Patrick, knowing the people put much emphasis on the number three, used the shamrock to illustrate the Trinity. Father, Son, and Holy Spirit are one God, just as the three-leafed shamrock is one plant. We don't know if St. Patrick actually did this, but it doesn't matter. The shamrock can serve as a Christian symbol no matter who thought of it.

Triquetra or Trinity Knot: Again, this is a symbol that has many meanings attributed to it, but for the Christian it, like the shamrock, represents the Trinity. The three interconnected ovals represent the power of three, unbreakable and strong.

The Celtic Knot or Braid: With no beginning or end, this symbol serves to remind me of God: *In the beginning*

51

the Word already existed. The Word was with God, and the Word was God. John 1:1 NLT And the Celtic knot also reminds me of this verse in Ecclesiastes: a triple-braided cord is not easily broken. Ecclesiastes 4:12 NLT

These are just a few examples. You may find more. The important thing is that when you look at these symbols you are reminded of a truth or of the nature of God, things that should not be forgotten.

> CHALLENGE: Choose one symbol to focus on. Draw it, print it out on paper, sew it on a garment—whatever you'd like, but keep it in front of you for several days and see if it serves to remind you of God and his promises.

> *Dear Father, help me to write your words on the doorposts of my heart. Amen.*

PART FIVE

LOVE

The love and affection of the angels be to you,
The love and affection of the saints be to you,
The love and affection of heaven be to you,
To guard you and to cherish you.
~From the Carmina Gadelica[16]

LOVE

Evening Seventeen

*Whoever does not love does not know God, because God
is love. 1 John 4:8 NIV*

The Celtic Christian monks had rules, many of which
survive for us to read today. Most were quite strict about
things such as diet, costume, religious ritual, and prayer times.
But there were other rules pertaining to hospitality and caring
for the poor. These acts were to show God's love because if a
believer did nothing to show God's love to others, he or she
did not truly know God. The seventh-century abbot of Rahan,
County Offaly, and founder of Lismore, Mochuda Raithin,
began his written rule with the Ten Commandments.[17] "Let all
people love God in heart and deed. To love God with all your
strength is not, as is obvious, a matter for sorrow. You are also
to love your neighbor as you love yourself."

The Rule attributed to sixth-century St. Comghall of
Bangor, puts it plainly: "In this lies the heart of the rule: to
love Christ ..." If we utilize this one rule, live by it, and write
these words on our hearts, all the rest will fall in line.

Augustine of Hippo, who lived from 354 – 430, was not a Celtic Christian. However, the Celtic Christians were influenced by the desert monks, or those living in Egypt. While Augustine is not one of these early influences — in fact he differed with Pelagius, a Celtic monk — Augustine was influenced by the desert fathers as well. He cites the written Life of one them, St. Antony, as leading to his conversion. As a Christian philosopher, Augustine is still widely quoted today. Whether or not we agree with all he said, it's certain he had a major influence on the Western Church. In all his writings there is perhaps nothing more important, and so often quoted from pulpits today, than the following. Augustine said, to paraphrase, "Love God and do as you please." Jesus also said as much when asked what the greatest commandment was. (Matthew 22:36-40)

> CHALLENGE: Think over the last twenty-four hours. Were your acts done out of love? How might things have changed had you decided to put love first?

> *Dear Father, help me to always love you first. I know that love will then shine through me to others as I love them more than myself. Your love is not selfish. Help mine to be unselfish as well. Amen.*

LOVE

Evening Eighteen

*Neither height nor depth, nor anything else in all
creation, will be able to separate us from the love of God
that is in Christ Jesus our Lord. Romans 8:39 NIV*

History tells us the Viking invasions in Ireland were
horrifying. These attacks took place mainly in the eighth and
ninth centuries, although a resurgence occurred in the first
half of the tenth century. The pillaging concentrated on
Christian settlements because monasteries were where the
churches were, and the churches kept gold liturgical elements
on their altars. Jewel-encrusted book shrines covered
ceremonial Bibles and cherished illuminated manuscripts.
Many times, the pages were ripped from the shrines and
thrown into the bogs because the raiders believed the insides
were of no value. The monastic centers offered more bounty
than could be found elsewhere on the island.

Eventually the monks found ways to defend
themselves. Most historians believe one method resulted in the
appearance of round towers all across the island. The remains

of sixty-five can still be seen today, some soaring a hundred feet tall. The door was placed high off the ground. The monks would use a ladder to climb in and then pull the ladder up behind them. Inside, each floor was constructed the same way. They used a ladder to ascend and then pulled the ladder up with them. In this way they were able to save some of their valuables and also their lives.[18]

The well-known hymn, *Be Thou My Vision*, comes from this era in Ireland. One of the verses likely reflects the use of round towers. There are several translations. The one below is by Eleanor Hull, 1912.

> *Be Thou my battle Shield,*
> *Sword for the fight;*
> *Be Thou my Dignity,*
> *Thou my Delight;*
> *Thou my soul's Shelter,*
> *Thou my high Tow'r:*
> *Raise Thou me heav'nward,*
> *O Pow'r of my pow'r.*

Despite those terrifying times, the Christians knew God was with them. His love could not be separated from them no matter where they found themselves. Knowing this would have brought great relief, as Romans 8:39 teaches. Perhaps they also meditated on this proverb: "The name of the Lord is a fortified tower; the righteous run to it and are safe."

Proverbs 18:10 NIV

CHALLENGE: Think of a time when God felt very far away. Imagine the strong, tall tower of his love encircling you, and vow to remember that image the next time you are tempted to feel apart from his love.

Dear Father, may I never forget that your love protects me no matter where I find myself. No danger can ever separate me from your love. Amen.

LOVE

Evening Nineteen

But I tell you, love your enemies and pray for those who persecute you. Matthew 5:44 NIV

This is one of the most difficult things Jesus told his followers to do in his Sermon on the Mount. And yet, it's there in black and white. We are supposed to do this. Jesus wants us to. I believe one of the reasons the Celtic Christians often isolated themselves was so that they could devote themselves to prayer. Prayer for their enemies, and for the enemies of all their fellow Irish. It was hard work, requiring a lot of time and attention. Eventually most of these hermits returned to face civilization. Monasteries were centers of learning and of trade, precursors to cities that were yet to be built in Ireland. The monks and other faithful followers of Christ had to eventually meet up with people who persecuted them, not unlike people today.

St. Columcille was one who faced persecution in the sixth century. When he went to Iona off the coast of Scotland to establish a monastery, he was met with some opposition.

61

The manner in which he converted the people he encountered likely echoed the ways of St. Patrick before him. He listened. He found the beliefs they already had and showed them the path to the One True God. Giving up multiple gods would not have been easy for the ancient tribes. There most certainly would have been a struggle. Conflict that Columcille and others faced down with prayer. They prayed for the souls of those who opposed them and eventually brought them to the Christian faith. That must have been the reason for Jesus' teaching. We cannot change hearts. Only God can do that. So pray for your enemies, love them, even when they torment, bully, or humiliate you.

St. Columban (Columbanus in Latin) is another example from the history of the Celtic Christians. This seventh-century missionary monk set up monasteries in Frankish and Italian kingdoms. Irish monks saw the church differently than those influenced by Rome. For them, bishops in the Roman church held no sway over an Irish abbot who ruled his monastery. This belief was easier to maintain in Ireland, and Columban faced opposition in the foreign lands. Rulers of the kingdoms grew suspicious of Columban's popularity among the people. The Roman church was static.

The Irish church moved around and reached out. He was expelled from France but continued establishing monasteries in the countryside and finished his work in Italy. I know of no record stating that Columban prayed for his enemies, but he certainly had them. Praying for others, even those you don't particularly like, was the Celtic Christian way. Moving toward those enemies was something those like Columcille and Columban, and Patrick before them did not fear. They understood that all people were to be loved, not just the ones closest to you.

CHALLENGE: Think of someone you don't particularly like and pray for them right now. Did the process of praying help you open your heart to them? If not, don't worry. Loving enemies is a process. Just keep praying.

Dear Father, it's hard to love those who persecute me. I know it's not hard for you. Give me your heart for those I find it hard to love. Keep reminding me that the people I find the most difficult to pray for need your love. Amen.

LOVE

Evening Twenty

If I could speak all the languages of earth and of angels, but didn't love others, I would only be a noisy gong or a clanging cymbal. 1 Corinthians 13:1 NLT

This chapter in Corinthians is the love chapter. In it we learn how important love is and that love comes from God. I want to focus on that first verse. Knowing all the languages of the world would take great intellect and wisdom. It would be a prodigious honor to speak the language of angels, wouldn't it? However, if you had that ability and didn't love your fellow human beings, your linguistic skills would be nothing but a lot of noise.

The ancient Celtic world was not necessarily a quiet place, not entirely. The era of St. Patrick was filled with wild beasts and other noises of the natural world. There was music (see my book *Celtic Song*) and there were great festivals at the turning of the seasons. Song, dance, laughter, disagreements, war. Many monasteries were overcrowded as people came there to learn and to live safely within the walls (except for during Viking raids, of course). If the early Christians only tended to the duties of providing sustenance, running markets, copying books, and never actually loved those they served, none of what they attempted to do would have been fruitful. Their efforts would have been nothing but the noise of a banging gong. Love was the key. It still is. Busyness can serve as a distraction. Even good mission work like feeding and educating the needy can come to nothing if love is not behind those actions.

Lady Gregory, a late nineteenth-century Irish folklorist, translated this piece attributed to St. Brigid from ancient texts:

I would wish the men of Heaven in my own house.

I would wish vessels of peace to be given to them.[19]

Vessels of peace. This is not real food or drink. This refers to something coming only from the wellspring of love. Peace of mind. Peace overflowing. What a wonderful image. What an incredible thing to wish for someone.

CHALLENGE: When you do something for someone, pause to examine your motives. Are you doing this thing because it makes you feel better or are you doing it out of love? If you do not like your answer, ask God to guide you.

Dear Father, I want to be more than just a clanging cymbal. Help me to do your work with the love you have shown me. Amen.

PART SIX

ACT

Endow me with strength,
Thou Herdsman of might,
Guide me aright,
Guide me in Thy strength
O Jesu! In Thy strength
Preserve me.
~From the Carmina Gadelica[20]

ACT

Evening Twenty-One

*But the Lord God warned him, "You may freely eat the
fruit of every tree in the garden except the tree of the
knowledge of good and evil. If you eat its fruit, you are
sure to die."*
Genesis 2:16-17 NLT

God's instruction to Adam and Eve was not to eat the
fruit of one particular tree. We all know what happened. They
did it. Temptation causes us to act in ways we know we
shouldn't. Paul, in his letter to the Romans understood this.
"For what I want to do I do not do, but what I hate I do."
Romans 7:15 NIV

Like all Christians, the early Celtic Christians faced
temptation. They, like all of us, had to choose how to act in
various circumstances. None of them was perfect, but enough
of them followed the way of Christ that leads to eternal life
that we are able to see the path.

St. Cuthbert, monk and bishop in the seventh century at
Lindisfarne in northern England, serves as a good example of
how to turn away from sins because he modeled it for his

followers. In Edward Sellner's book, **Wisdom of the Celtic Saints**, he says Culthbert, "...readily challenged wrongdoers because of his thirst for justice." Sellner says the saint would often burst into tears of compassion when hearing the confession of sins. And then Culthbert would do a remarkable thing, something that must have had a great impact on the people. "Though he [Culthbert] himself did not need to do so, he would show them how to make recompense for their sins by doing the penance himself."[21]

Taking on the punishment for someone else's sin. The Bible tells us that because of Adam and Eve's sin, they became separated from God. Jesus took on the sin of humans to open that path back up. A mistake (sin) was made in the garden, but there was a solution through the cross (forgiveness.) Culthbert did not die on a cross, but he took up the cross. He followed Christ's example by showing his followers the way, not just talking about it or preaching a good sermon, but by walking through the pain with them.

> CHALLENGE: You know someone who is in pain. Think about that until compassion fills your heart. What action might you take that will show him/her the way?
>
> *Dear Father, help me to feel what others feel, even if their actions caused the pain they are experiencing right now.*

Help me to feel the sorrow you feel. Only by acknowledging the difficult journey can I light the path to you. Help me to act rather than lecture. Love rather than despise. Serve rather than stand by idly. Amen.

ACT

Evening Twenty-Two

And you must love the Lord your God with all your heart, all your soul, and all your strength. Deuteronomy 6:5 NLT

You must love, and completely. This is not an option, but it certainly is a difficult directive in some circumstances. What might that look like in action? Again, taking a look at the example of the early Celtic world, it certainly embodied hospitality. P.W. Joyce, a nineteenth-century Irish historian, tells us that, "Hospitality and generosity were virtues highly esteemed in ancient Ireland … The higher the rank of the person the more was expected from him, and a king should be lavish without limit."[22] The Venerable Bede, in his *Ecclesiastical History of the English People*, penned in the early eighth century noted the remarkable benevolence and hospitality of the Irish monks.

Jesus in his parables said, "Truly I tell you, whatever you did for one of the least of these brothers and sisters of mine, you did for me." Matthew 25:40 NIV God doesn't need us to provide for him, but he does desire for us to do what we can for others. If this is the motivation, as it was for the early Celtic Christians, then it becomes an act of love for God.

CHALLENGE: Do one thing today for someone, even a small act of kindness, without identifying yourself as the giver. Do it out of your love for God.

Dear Father, I know I cannot care for all of the needy people in the world. Help me to make one step, one act of giving, keeping my thoughts on you alone. Amen.

ACT

Evening Twenty-Three

Don't let anyone treat him with contempt. Send him on his way with your blessing when he returns to me. I expect him to come with the other believers. 1 Corinthians 16:11 NLT

In this verse Paul is speaking to the Corinthians, instructing them to bless Timothy. The practice of blessing someone, especially when sending him or her on his way, is a powerful act Christians can do for others. The ancient Irish were always offering blessings. When entering a house they would voice a blessing to all who dwelt there. Blessings were spoken for every activity.

The *Carmina Gadelica* is filled with such blessings. Here is a portion of one titled "Reaping Blessing."

God, bless Thou Thyself my reaping,

Each ridge, and plain, and field,

Each sickle curved, shapely, hard,

Each ear and handful in the sheaf,

Each ear and handful in the sheaf.

Blessings were always spoken before traveling, such as this example titled "Sea Prayer."

> Blest be the boat,
> God the Father bless her.
> Blest be the boat,
> God the Spirit bless her.
> Blest be the boat,
> God the Spirit bless her.
> God the Father,
> God the Son,
> God the Holy Spirt,
> Bless the boat.
> What can befall you
> And God the Father with you?
> No harm can befall us.[23]

Why is the act of blessing so important? I like the way Christine Valters Paintner put it in her book, *The Soul's Slow Ripening*. "Blessing is really acknowledging the gifts and graces already present and entering into partnership with the divine."[24]

CHALLENGE: Speak a blessing over someone who comes to mind right now, whether silently or in their hearing. Think about what that means to both the subject of the blessing and God who has instructed you to do so.

Dear Father, keep me ever mindful of speaking blessings during the mundane activities of daily life and in light of important journeys. Thank you for blessing me. Amen.

ACT

Evening Twenty-Four

*You must each decide in your heart how much to give.
And don't give reluctantly or in response to pressure.
"For God loves a person who gives cheerfully." 2
Corinthians 9:7 NLT*

In your act of giving there should be no compulsion, no guilt, no pressure from anyone. The stories of the ancient Christian saints are filled with examples of cheerful giving. St. Brigid is a good model of this. She was known to give away whatever she had when she saw someone in need. Her father was not as keen about her giving, and since he could not compel her to stop, he made up his mind to put her into the king's service. He shouldn't have been so annoyed because everything she gave away from the dairy where she worked was miraculously restored. Brigid's father was not a believer, however, so he probably feared his wealth would one day disappear if he didn't do something. Brigid waited in the chariot while her father sought an audience with the king. A beggar approached her, asking for help. Away from the dairy, she was at a loss for what to give him until she spotted her father's sword in the back of the chariot. This was no ordinary sword. With a jewel-encrusted hilt, the weapon was very valuable. Even so, the sword was the only thing available at that moment, so Brigid handed it over. Her father and the king emerged from the castle just in time to see the beggar rush away with the sword. "You see," Brigid's father said. "I must be rid of her before she gives away everything I own."

The king, being wise as kings are always considered to be, questioned Brigid about what she had done. In response Brigid waved her arm toward the king's lush green fields and abundance of grazing cattle. "If I owned all that you do, that's how much and no less I would give to those starving people." The king felt humbled by this declaration and instead of taking Brigid into his household he granted her freedom. Brigid gave it all away, believing none of it belonged to her or her father or even the king. Every good thing comes from above, as the writer of James said.

Cancer took away a good friend of mine too soon. Her husband was a successful businessman, and by most standards they were wealthy. However, money and material possessions didn't matter to her. She was constantly sharing with family and friends. She told me once that her husband told her to be mindful of the difference in what people wanted and what they needed. Her brother needed some dental care he could not afford. She told her husband that her brother *needed* it and she *wanted* to give it to him. She was an example of faith in action: caring, loving, serving, and blessing someone. Her example has stayed with me and also, I'm sure, with all who had known her. Not because she had money and gave things away, but because she held nothing back, believing none of it was truly hers anyway. You don't need a lot of money to put this kind of faith into action, just an attitude of wanting to give. A generous heart easily discovers opportunities.

> I have no love for wealth,
> Its trace is always passing.
> I am God's servant; highest praise to him,
> The God it is best to follow.

~From the Welsh poem *The Song of Elafth*, translated by Oliver Davies[25]

CHALLENGE: Begin to release all worldly possessions to God, the giver of all good things. As you begin to view money and belongings in this light, how will your ability to be generous change?

Dear Father, help me to be a cheerful giver of things, of time, of compassion. Show me the ways I might give to others right now. Amen.

PART SEVEN

GUIDE

*Steer the ship of my life, good Lord, to your quiet
harbour, where I can be safe from the storms of sin and
conflict. Show me the course I should take. Renew in me
the gift of discernment, so that I can always see the right
direction in which I should go. And give me the strength
and the courage to choose the right course, even when the
sea is rough and the waves are high, knowing that
through enduring hardship and danger we shall find
comfort and peace.*

~Saint Basil of Caesarea[26]

GUIDE

Evening Twenty-Five

*Guide me in your truth and teach me, for you are God
my Savior, and my hope is in you all day long. Psalm
25:5 NIV
I on Thy path, O God
Thou, O God, in my steps.
(From the Carmina Gadelica)[27]*

While I firmly believe we can learn much from the
voices of the past, it's ultimately God we look to for guidance.
Our Christian ancestors did as we are to do. They looked to
those who went before them as examples of how to follow
Christ.

Alone with none but Thee, my God,
I journey on my way;
What need I fear when Thou art near,
Oh King of night and day?
More safe am I within Thy hand
Than if a host did round me stand.
~Attributed to St. Columba

Columcille (or Columba in Latin) looked for God's
guidance as he led his fellow monks. Beginning at a young
age, he followed not the path that would have been expected

of him but God's plan for his life instead. From my book, ***The Roots of Irish Wisdom***: "Columcille was wealthy and privileged, presumably in line to be High King had he not chosen the religious life."[28] Columcille founded numerous monasteries, including Iona off the coast of Scotland, perhaps the best known of all of them. He loved books and continued transcribing (the only the way books were shared then) almost until the very last. His influence was vast and long lasting, much more of an enduring legacy than being High King would have been. He instructed his followers to keep looking to God, even on his deathbed when he told them, "… if you thus follow the example of the holy fathers, God, the Comforter of the good, will be your Helper …"

> CHALLENGE: Think about how willing you are to be guided. If there is any self-will holding you back, decide to turn away from it.

> *Dear Father, be my guide and the light on my path. Help me to always look to you and not to my own understanding as I journey on my way. Amen.*

GUIDE

Evening Twenty-Six

The Lord will guide you always; he will satisfy your needs in a sun-scorched land and will strengthen your frame. You will be like a well-watered garden, like a spring whose waters never fail. Isaiah 58:11 NIV

The kind of analogy with nature that Isaiah uses would have resonated with the ancient Celtic people. St. Columcille is credited with saying, "If you want to know the Creator, understand creation."

George MacLeod was a minister, poet, and Celtic Christian born in Scotland in 1895. In the 1930s he began rebuilding the ancient abbey at Iona, the site most associated with St. Columcille, and launched the modern Iona community, which is described as "a multi-denominational religious community dedicated to restoring the early Christian church buildings on the island and to furthering the case for ecumenicalism."[29] He traveled a different path than the established church he ministered through, choosing to do so by listening for God's guidance.

From one of MacLeod's poems:

87

Almighty God, Creator:
The morning is Yours, rising into fullness.
The summer is Yours, dipping into autumn.
Eternity is Yours, dipping into time.
The vibrant grasses, the scent of flowers, the lichen on the
Rocks, the tan of seaweed.
All are Yours.
Gladly we live in this garden of Your creating.

A well-watered garden, as Isaiah says. We all want to be led there, the Garden of Eden of our souls, the place we're meant to be. Isaiah had some trouble convincing the Israelites of this. How often do we think there are greener pastures out there and we need to go locate them? All we find is a sun-scorched land.

The ancient Celtic monks were greatly influenced by the desert fathers of Egypt who knew what a sun-scorched land was like. The Christians in Celtic lands may not have lived in a desert environment, but they knew harsh conditions. Perhaps this is why they so greatly appreciated the beauty surrounding them. Weather could change suddenly, famine could hit, and the plague and other devastating illnesses were ever present. Where was God? Waiting to lead them to the lushness of life, painting rainbows of promise in the sky.

CHALLENGE: What unique path might God be calling you to? Make a list of the obstacles you see and think of ways God might be leading you around them and through them.

Dear Father, you are the Creator of the natural world. Help me to appreciate what is around me while listening for your guidance. I trust that you will guide me to the garden where I will gladly dwell. Amen.

GUIDE

Evening Twenty-Seven

*But when he, the Spirit of truth, comes, he will guide you
into all the truth. He will not speak on his own; he will
speak only what he hears, and he will tell you what is yet
to come. John 16:13 NIV*

When Jesus died and ascended into heaven, he did not
leave his followers alone. The Holy Spirit, the Spirit of Truth,
remained to guide them and those who came after. It was the
Holy Spirit that prompted St. Patrick to return to Ireland to
minister to the Irish. It was the Holy Spirit that led Columcille
to Iona. It was the Holy Spirit that sent St. Brenden off in a
rudderless boat to find a place that was only known through
legend. And it was the Holy Spirit that guided a monk named
Canice to pray for his friend, St. Columcille. Columcille was at
that moment navigating through a dangerous storm at sea.
Canice felt the need to pray so urgently that it's said he ran to
the church wearing only one shoe.

The concept of the Holy Spirit guiding one into truth
was embraced by the Irish, and still is by many. When
someone dies the idea of moving from one life to the next is

91

described in the Irish phrase: *slí na fírinne,* which translates as *the path to truth.* It occurs to me that we are on that path as soon as we arrive on earth. Those who pass on are truly on their way and no longer wandering a route that is most times difficult to discern. The path to truth is the path the Holy Spirit leads us toward, guiding our way.

> CHALLENGE: Consider whether you are on the right path right now. Make it a point to seek guidance from the Spirit of Truth.

> *Dear Father, thank you for sending your Spirit. I draw comfort from knowing I am never alone even though at times I have no idea where I am. Guide me on the path to truth. Amen.*

GUIDE

Evening Twenty-Eight

Very early in the morning, while it was still dark, Jesus
got up, left the house and went off to a solitary place,
where he prayed. Mark 1:35 NIV

Jesus led by example as well as teaching. He taught us

to pray, both the words themselves (commonly known as The

Lord's Prayer) and in the manner in which to pray. In this

passage in Mark, Jesus had been healing people and

performing miracles. The whole town was at his door. How

can someone keep up that pace? By seeking strength from

God, of course, through prayer and quiet contemplation. But

the place where Jesus ministered was crowded with people

who all wanted something from him. He had to get up before

everyone awoke to sneak away and pray.

> Jesu, from today
> Guide us on our way,
> So shall we, no moment wasting,
> Follow Thee with holy hasting,
> Led by Thy dear Hand
> To the Blessed Land.

~From *The Celtic Psaltery* by Alfred Perceval Graves[30]

When Patrick was a slave in Ireland, he spent many days alone tending livestock out in the wind and rain. He had time to ponder his life and eventually used this time to pray, which he then did a lot, as often as a hundred times at night and again during the day. He wrote: "And there the Lord opened my mind to an awareness of my unbelief … he watched over me before I knew him, and before I learned sense or even distinguished between good and evil, and he protected me, and consoled me as a father would his son."[31]

Patrick may not have known it at the time, but he was being led by Jesus' example. Guided to a quiet place and encouraged to pray. It changed Patrick's life.

CHALLENGE: Make it a point to get away somewhere quiet. Read the first chapter of Mark and consider how Jesus is guiding you through his example.

Dear Father, I get caught up in the busyness of life and forget that I need to pray and listen. Remind me. Wake me if necessary. Let me never forsake speaking with you through prayer. Amen.

PART EIGHT

CELEBRATE

It is good to praise the LORD,
And make music to your name, O Most High.
~Psalm 92:1 NIV

CELEBRATE

Evening Twenty-Nine

This is a day you are to commemorate; for the
generations to come you shall celebrate it as a festival to
the Lord—a lasting ordinance. Exodus 12:14 NIV

Festivals are some of my favorite events, especially Irish or Celtic festivals. Celebrations should be a part of life. The passage in Exodus is referring to the Passover, the time when the angel of death passed over the houses of the Israelites and spared the firstborn sons judgment. The people prayed, they were faithful in following the instructions Moses and Aaron gave them, and God was faithful too. That is reason to celebrate.

The ancient Celtic people observed a calendar based on the seasons. Samhain was and is the festival marking the dark half of the year. People would dress up and light bonfires. Christians observed All Saints Day on November 1 and the evening before became known as All Hallowed Eve, or Halloween. The worlds of the living and the dead pass close together, in the belief of the ancient people. Feasting would have been common this time of year as it was time to butcher livestock that would not be overwintered and time to bring in the harvest of the fields. Imbolc marked the coming of the light half of the year. This also marks the feast of St. Brigid, who was named for the goddess of fire who brought light to the darkness. Beltane is the festival beginning in May, the start of summer and the beginning of growth. Then Lammas comes, the festival of harvest, in August. Thus the Celtic year is divided in half, the dark and the light, and then those are again divided in half with summer and fall (May and August.) It's not difficult to see how the coming of the church adopted some of these festivals and observances and turned them into Christian celebrations. There is a legend about just that involving St. Patrick, who was on the Hill of Slane when the king ordered all fires to be put out so that his festival fire would be the only one seen for miles.

I have visited Slane. It indeed is a site high on top of a hill where you can see the landscape below in all directions. The view is spectacular and you should visit if you have the opportunity. The importance of the site dates well before Christianity and even before the Celts arrived. There are ancient burial sites nearby and a well considered to have healing abilities. The earthworks and passage tombs are prehistoric. Ancient people worshipped on the hill and claimed it as a sacred site. Today a St. Patrick statue stands to commemorate the story alongside Christian ruins and graves. Some archeologists believe the event involving St. Patrick did not happen at Slane but elsewhere in the Boyne Valley. However, it's easy to imagine it at the Hill of Slane, a spot where a fire in the dark of night could be seen all over the valley. The king's fire was to be lit on the Spring Equinox. The equinoxes were also marked and observed. Such passage tombs as Newgrange (also in the Boyne Valley) were built to accommodate the first ray of sun on those days. Patrick and his followers were traveling through and stopped at Slane to light a Paschal fire. They did so despite the king's orders and were chased down. They weren't caught, however, because the Christians were turned into deer and escaped safely. A loose comparison could be made to the Passover. The Christians were faithful to celebrate a religious rite and were saved from harm. This event at Slane marked the beginning of the island converting to the faith.

CHALLENGE: What festivals do you celebrate? Make a point to observe God's goodness in light of all the days of celebrating.

Dear Father, I celebrate you and your love. Help me to make that plain in the eyes of others. Help me to remember your holy days with great rejoicing. Amen.

CELEBRATE

Evening Thirty

But we had to celebrate and be glad, because this brother of yours was dead and is alive again; he was lost and is found. Luke 15:32 NIV

The parable of the prodigal son is one of the most complex and powerful stories in the Gospels. I realized this reading Henri Nouwen's *The Return of the Prodigal Son.* Nouwen was long fascinated with Rembrandt's painting of the same name even before he saw the actual painting in St. Petersburg at the Hermitage Museum. You know the story. A second-born son asked his father for his inheritance instead of waiting for his father to die. He ran away to a far country and squandered it all. He was forced to take work as a farmhand, and when he realized what he fed to the pigs looked pretty good to him, he returned home planning to ask to become a servant for his father because they were treated better than the life he now had. The father welcomed him home, killed the fatted calf, had a party. The older brother was miffed. He'd been loyal and his father never killed the fatted calf for him. The father's response is the verse above.

The unconditional love of the Father is what speaks to most of us about this verse. It reminds me of the Celtic concept of sanctuary. Some believe high crosses once marked the boundaries of the monasteries. Once a person crossed into their shadow, no matter what they might have done or who might be pursuing them, they were safe from harm within the confines of the Christian community, not because the religious people were there but because God was the true host and the church his house. The Irish word *termonn* refers to this practice and translates as sanctuary or boundary. The communities contained guesthouses where visitors were welcomed and indeed expected. The concept of sanctuary can be viewed as a sort of homecoming, safe in the Father's arms, just like the image in Rembrandt's painting.

While a safe homecoming is a satisfying end to the story, the parable does not stop there. There is celebration, rejoicing, and feasting. Most people know how to have a party, but what we are celebrating might not always be as clear as in this story. What was lost is found. What was dead lives again. This can only be accomplished within the boundaries of sanctuary where God is the host.

CHALLENGE: Are you the younger son in this story or the older son? What can you do to move more toward the role of the father?

Dear Father, I am so grateful that you welcome me home no matter how many mistakes I've made. Help me to celebrate this in myself and in others. Help me to extend the celebration to all who return to you. Amen.

CELEBRATE

Evening Thirty-One

They celebrate your abundant goodness and joyfully sing of your righteousness. Psalm 145:4 NIV

We are to celebrate God's abundant goodness. The Christians in the Celtic lands understood this.

There is no bird on the wing,

There is no star in the sky,

There is nothing beneath the sun,

But proclaims His goodness.

Jesu! Jesu! Jesu!

From *Jesu Who Ought to Be Praised* in the *Carmina Gadelica*[32]

Goodness is one of the fruits of the Spirit. It is God's goodness that we seek to emulate. The ancient Celtic saints strove to be good to others by constantly offering advice, aid to the hungry and homeless, and comfort to those in distress. Author Edward Sellner says this of St. Brendan: "...after raising dead men, healing lepers, the blind, deaf, and lame ... after founding many cells, monasteries, and churches ...

105

performing mighty works and miracles too numerous to mention, Brendan drew near to the day of his death."[33] Being good in the Christian sense was a never-ending endeavor requiring at times much sacrifice. Jesus told us the poor would always be with us. The job is never finished and is passed on to younger generations. Our goodness is limited by our human restraints and yet the psalmist tells us God has abundant goodness and we should celebrate his righteousness with singing.

We don't know the melodies the ancient Celtic Christian employed, but we do know the celebration of music was a part of their lives. I explore this in my book ***Celtic Song: From the Traditions of Ireland, Scotland, England, and Wales.*** One can only imagine the deep sense of worship they experienced while celebrating. Let us celebrate as they must have.

CHALLENGE: Find a song or melody that speaks to your soul. As you listen, celebrate God's goodness and ask the Holy Spirit to let goodness flow through your actions and words.

Dear Father, everything you created is good. I want to be good to others. Instruct me as you did the ancient Christians. Help me to celebrate this in everything I do and say. Amen.

CELEBRATE

Evening Thirty-Two

Vast supplies of flour, fig cakes, clusters of raisins, wine, olive oil, cattle, sheep, and goats were brought to the celebration. There was great joy throughout the land of Israel. 1 Chronicles 12:40 NLT

This verse comes at the end of the tribes choosing David as their new king. It describes food as being a part of the celebration. We know that the ancient monasteries in the Celtic lands were austere places. Some only partook of bread and water for many days. They were allowed meat and ale on feast days and on Easter. However, St. Brigid is associated with more abundant feasting. She gave away great quantities of food. She famously wished for a great lake of beer from which all of the saints in heaven would partake.

> I would wish a great lake of ale for the King of Kings;
> I would wish the family of heaven to be drinking it
> throughout life and time.
> I would wish the men of Heaven in my own house;
> I would wish vessels of peace to be given to them.
> I would wish joy to be in their drinking;
> I would wish Jesu to be here among them.[34]

Fasting played a role in the lives of these Celts but so did feasting. If the Israelites celebrated in such a fashion the knowledge that David would be king, shouldn't we celebrate the King of Kings? Whether by way of a great lake of ale or a mountain of fig cakes or some other treat, we must celebrate "great joy throughout the land."

> CHALLENGE: Make something special to celebrate the King and think about how wondrous it is that God loves you and celebrates with you.

> *Dear Father, I celebrate the life you gave me and the assurance that one day I will join the great feast in heaven with all the saints. Thank you for the joy of celebration. Amen.*

PART NINE

HOPE

*My soul quietly waits for the True God alone because I
hope only in Him.
~Psalm 62:5 VOICE*

HOPE

Evening Thirty-Three

*We can rejoice, too, when we run into problems and
trials, for we know that they help us develop endurance.
And endurance develops strength of character, and
character strengthens our confident hope of salvation.*
Romans 5:3-4 NLT

Hild of Whitby, a well-known female Anglo-Saxon
saint in the medieval Celtic region of northern England and
southeastern Scotland called Northumbria was abbess during
the great dispute over the date of Easter and other issues
between Celtic and Roman Christians known as the Synod of
Whitby in 664. While she is known to have been on the Irish
Celtic side of the dispute and was a woman of stern influence,
what stands out to me most about her is how she endured a
long sickness. In Edward Sellner's book, **Wisdom of the Celtic
Saints**, he says she suffered from an illness that included high
fevers, and this condition lasted the last seven years of her life.
He says she continued to praise God and admonish those with
good health to serve the Lord. In her final year she was in
great pain and on her death bed she urged her followers to,

111

"... preserve the gospel peace among themselves and toward all others. While still exhorting them, she joyfully saw death approach or rather, to use the words of the Lord, she 'passed from death into life.'"[35]

Many of us know saints like this. I think of a few I have known who suffered mightily but never gave up their faith. People like that leave an enormous impression on those who witness the closing years, months, or days of these people's lives. It's comforting to know there have been numerous examples of people who have exhibited this type of influence throughout the ages. Without such examples would we fully grasp the meaning of grace? Would faith in Christ survive without their legacy? People like Hild of Whitby shine light on the hope of salvation. Christians like her show us that suffering has a purpose: it strengthens our endurance and leads us to the hope of heaven.

CHALLENGE: Think of someone who, despite challenges of illness or life circumstances, has made an influence on your spiritual life. How might you exhibit the same kind of character to those around you?

Dear Father, thank you for giving me endurance and strengthening me for the trials I face. Like the saints of old, such endurance only comes from faith in you. Thank you for giving me hope to hang on to through all sorts of turmoil. Amen.

HOPE

Evening Thirty-Four

But the needy will not be ignored forever; the hopes of the poor will not always be crushed. Psalm 9:18 NLT

Our spirits can easily be crushed. We are inclined toward despair far too frequently. This psalm reminds us it won't always be this way. Even when the world ignores us, God remembers.

During my first trip to Ireland my father passed away. As I boarded the flight to Dublin, I felt his passing loomed nearer than I had realized. Looking back, I should have known, but I didn't want to acknowledge it at the time. I found the idea of life without him difficult to comprehend. At the airport, however, reality hit me. Over the phone my dad told me it was good I was going. He said he loved me, and then he said something that made it all real.

My father was a part of the Greatest Generation, a child when the Great Depression hit, and a teen when Pearl Harbor was attacked. At seventeen he enlisted in the U.S. Navy. He saw combat in the South Pacific for nearly two straight years with very little respite. After the war he got married on impulse, and after a few years decided the military offered the best opportunity for employment so he signed up for the army. All told twenty years in the military trained him to be tough and resilient. He was raised, as most men of that era were, to show little emotion, especially toward other men. He loved deeply but would never hug another man, let alone verbalize any affection. He embraced my husband, but without any mushy stuff. When we draw close to the end of our lives, we tend to give up all pretense. That day on the phone in the Philadelphia airport, I listened as my father told me to tell my husband that he loved him too. That crushed me. After I hung up, I felt God speak to my spirit, asking me what I was afraid of. Passing to new life, to the garden our souls long for, is good, is it not? My crushed spirit rallied. God had heard my pain and brought comfort.

Esther deWaal devotes a chapter in her book, *The Celtic Way of Prayer*, to darkness, pain, and suffering. She says the Celtic people have survived all that through the ages. "Out of their long experience of living under threat, the Celtic nations remind us to 'expect the morning light.'"[36]

Sunshine always follows rain. ~Irish Proverb

CHALLENGE: Light a candle and contemplate the hope a single candle exemplifies. If you feel despair now or have in the past, focus on the light and see it as a promise from God.

Dear Father, in dark times it's easy to forget this life is fleeting and therefore you will make my sorrows disappear. When I'm tempted to fall into despair, remind me of your light and the hope of heaven. Amen.

HOPE

Evening Thirty-Five

As for me, I will always have hope; I will praise you more and more.
Psalm 71:14 NIV

Meriam-Webster defines hope this way: desire accompanied by expectation of or belief in fulfillment. This definition almost sounds fleeting. Desires can come and go. The psalmist, however, declares that he will always have hope. That is why he praises God "more and more."

When I think about the examples of the ancient Celtic Christians, I marvel at how resolute they were in their faith. While occasional doubt is to be expected, they pushed through and kept on praising God because hope for them was their lifeline. As we have seen thus far, these people praised God constantly through a love of nature, regular prayer times, songs and poetry, and by caring for a flock of believers, those seeking Christ: the poor, the lonely, and all those looking for sanctuary.

119

While working on my novel ***Brigid of Ireland***, I often referenced a guidebook written by Conrad Blady for use in Catholic classrooms. Blady uses an alternative spelling of Brigid in this section, quoting from a nineteenth-century publication called *The Martyrology of Donegal, A Calendar of the Saints of Ireland*. "Brighit was following the manners and the life which the holy Mary, mother of Jesus had. It was this Brighit too, that did not take her mind or her attention from the Lord for the space of one hour ... but was constantly mentioning Him, and ever constantly thinking of Him, as evident in her own life..."[37]

There are two things about this description of Brigid that stand out to me. First, Jesus was constantly on her mind and she constantly spoke of him. That's continual praise. Second, these words: "as evident in her own life." There is no better witness to others than exhibiting what God has done for you. If others see through your words and actions that God has transformed you, they are more likely to believe such a change is possible for themselves.

> CHALLENGE: Write down your daily activities in a journal. Ask yourself if the presence of God is evident to others by the way you lived your life today. What might you do differently in light of this challenge?

Dear Father, I want to constantly praise you in all I do and all I think about. I fall short, but I am always hoping to do better, and I know you are the source of that hope. Thank you, Jesus! Amen.

HOPE

Evening Thirty-Six

*Such things were written in the Scriptures long ago to
teach us. And the Scriptures give us hope and
encouragement as we wait patiently for God's promises
to be fulfilled.*
Romans 15:4 NLT

While the ancient Celts learned about God through the
natural world, they also valued scripture, so much so they
devoted countless hours to copying it and illustrating it for
others. In the early Christian period in Ireland, books were
rare. The only way to share widely what was written "long
ago to teach us" was to make copies. The work of the scribe
was significant and sacred. These words encouraged and gave
hope just as they did when Paul wrote his letter to the
Romans.

There is a famous poem created by an Irish monk, in the
Irish language, likely in the eighth or ninth century in a
monastery in Austria. It's a lighthearted poem about a white
cat whose job is hunting mice. The cat is called Pangur Ban, in
Irish White Cat. The poem goes back and forth comparing the

cat's tasks to the scribe's. The last lines, translated by Robin Flower, read:

> Practice every day has made
>
> Pangur perfect in his trade;
>
> I get wisdom day and night
>
> Turning darkness into light.[38]

That sounds like an incredible responsibility, turning darkness into light. And the benefit to transcribing so much scripture is the scribe learned as he worked and grew wiser. This wisdom we can only assume gave the monk encouragement and hope for the life to come.

CHALLENGE: Spend some time transcribing a scripture passage of your choice. Imagine the ancient monk doing the same, passing along hope. Spend a few moments contemplating the significance of the ancient scribes.

Dear Father, thank you for the gift of scripture. Thank you for those who made sure the texts were preserved for the rest of us to give us hope. Your words are nourishment for my soul. Amen.

PART TEN

BEGIN

My genesis is in you, O God,
My beginnings are in Eden ...
Restore me to the truthfulness of my birth in you.
~J. Philip Newell[39]

BEGIN

Evening Thirty-Seven

Reverence for the Eternal is the first step toward wisdom.
All those who worship Him have a good understanding.
His praise will echo through eternity! Psalm 111:10
VOICE

As we wind up this devotional, it's time to talk about
how to begin the next step in our spiritual journey. I like this
modern translation of this psalm because it speaks about a first
step. Reverence for God. Some translations use the easily
confused word "fear." Merriam-Webster defines reverence
this way: honor or respect felt or shown, deference, profound
adoring awed respect. If that embodies your view of God, then
you have taken a step in the right direction. It's not fear as we
traditionally think of the word, but an awe and respect for
God's power.

The Skelligs off the west coast of Ireland are two rocky,
steep, seemingly uninhabitable islands. The smaller one is a
bird sanctuary and closed to the public. The larger one might
look familiar if you've seen the Star Wars episodes *The Force
Awakens* and *The Last Jedi*. This island portrayed Luke

Skywalker's hideaway on a remote planet. In real life one of the best-preserved examples of early Christian monastic living is found on this island. Tourists may visit the larger island, Skellig Michael, but only on good weather days. The island is isolated, stormy, and probably the loneliest place one could imagine despite being only eight miles off the coast of Ireland. The monks who lived there centuries ago left behind their beehive-shaped stone huts, stone monuments, and stone walls that encircled lofty terraces where, having lugged seaweed up cliffs for fertilizer, the monks gardened. They built 600 stone steps they must have traversed daily, going down to fish in the ocean and up again to return home. The top towers 714 feet over the Atlantic Ocean. Skellig Michael is not for those with a fear of heights or weak knees. Why live there? There were easier and more accessible places for the hermit monks to go for seclusion. Actually, the difficulty may have been the point. Arduous labor and isolation were thought to bring one closer to dependency on the Creator. There may have been another reason as well. In the wildest of places where storms lash and wildlife abounds, the majesty of God is distinctly evident and quite personal.

You may not ever visit Skellig Michael, but you may have gone through a very dark time during which you became acutely aware of the almighty and powerful God. This may have happened because you drew near to him through prayer. In the book of James we are told, "Come near to God and he will come near to you." (James 4:8 NIV) A couple of verses later we are told that if we humble ourselves, God will lift us up. Wherever your Skellig Michael might be, or in the future will be, remember that first step of wisdom and remember your awe-inspired reverence for the Maker.

> CHALLENGE: Think of a time when you felt complete wonder as you observed the power of God. It may have been the birth of a child, the sight of a vivid rainbow, the thunderous roar of a waterfall. Remember that feeling and draw on it during the times you feel a great need to be closer to God.

> *Dear Father, help me take that first step of wonder and reverence. Remind me that although this is just a beginning, it's one I need to experience. Thank you for being a God who inspires awe and respect. Amen.*

BEGIN

Evening Thirty-Eight

From that time on Jesus began to preach, "Repent, for the kingdom of heaven has come near." Matthew 4:17 NIV

After Jesus faced temptation from Satan in the wilderness, and after John the Baptist was arrested, Jesus began his ministry. (If you need a reminder of this story, read the entire fourth chapter of Matthew.) It was after this he called his disciples. He was about thirty years old according to the Gospel of Luke. Because of his divine nature, Jesus could have begun earlier. There were plenty of people who needed help both physically and spiritually. He could have begun earlier, but the time was not right. Some biblical scholars speculate that Jesus waited until such a time as the people would deem him mature and wise enough to warrant leadership. We don't really know. What we do know is Jesus began at the time God wanted him to. We'd like God to sign on to our timetables, wouldn't we? However, God's timing is perfect.

St. Ciaran of Saighir is sometimes referred to as Ireland's first native born saint. Because he lived much earlier than most of the early Christian saints in Ireland, this Ciaran (not to be confused with the later Ciaran of Clonmacnoise) may have known St. Patrick. There is a legend that Patrick sent him out to found monasteries with little in the way of precise directions where they should be located. Patrick gave him a bell and when the bell rang—solely by the will of God— Ciaran would know he'd arrived at the correct location. As with most Irish legends, there is a deeper meaning. What mattered was obedience. The saint was not to lean on his own understanding. He could not decide on his own based on the availability of natural resources, the distance away from unfriendly tribes, the availability of food. Ciaran had to take his own preferences out of the decision and listen to what God wanted and follow his plan for the timing and location of where Ciaran's ministry was to begin. This saint wore animal skins and communed with the wild animals, reminiscent of the biblical John the Baptist. Perhaps Ciaran's role was to set up Patrick's ministry, echoing John the Baptist's heralding of Jesus' work on earth.

This tale is not about ignoring the good sense God gave you. We do need to reason and make the best decisions we can. However, major decisions should not be made until we've taken the time to pray and listen and discern the direction of the bell, the metaphorical voice of God.

> CHALLENGE: Make a list of decisions you will need to make in the future, or a list of major decisions in which you have sought spiritual guidance in advance. Focus on one and commit to spending time in prayer and silent contemplation before you make that decision or if you've already done this think about that process. How did this decision affect the outcome?

> *Dear Father, I want to follow your timeline rather than one I create without your help. Help me to listen for your guidance, consult with godly advisors, and listen before I act. Your timing is perfect, and I know you will show me when to begin just as you showed Jesus. Amen.*

BEGIN

Evening Thirty-Nine

*Gather all the people—the elders, the children, and even
the babies. Call the bridegroom from his quarters and the
bride from her private room. Let the priests, who
minister in the Lord's presence, stand and weep between
the entry room to the Temple and the altar.
Let them pray, "Spare your people, Lord!" Joel 2:16-17
NLT*

The prophet Joel called God's people to repent. What
should God's people do when everything's a mess? Yes, listen
for his guidance, but to begin, repent and ask for salvation. An
important part of St. Columcille's legacy is the story of why he
left Ireland for Iona. By this time he had set up many
monasteries and had a great many followers. His influence
was vast, probably due in part to his social status. He was part
of the Uí Néill, the most powerful tribe in the north of Ireland.
An Cathach is a sixth-century psalter said to be hastily written
by Columcille. The story of how that book was written comes
from the fact that Columcille coveted a Vulgate copy of the
Psalms. The Vulgate is believed to be the first Latin translation
of the Bible from the fourth century, a valuable treasure in

Columcille's day. The owner, Columcille's former teacher, would not allow him to copy it so Columcille snuck into the library at night. He was able to make a copy because his fingers glowed like candles. This deceit was uncovered. A book becomes less valuable when a copy is made so the judges of the day ordered the copy to be returned to the owner of the original, ruling: To every cow its calf, to every book its copy. Columcille was so angered by this (his name means Dove of the Church, which was likely given him mockingly because he was known to have a temper) that he called on his powerful tribe to wage war. His side won but the cost was great. Columcille's tribe lost but one man in battle but the other side lost thousands. In his grief he banished himself (or was given the penance by his confessor) to Iona where he was just far enough away not to be able to glimpse his beloved Ireland. Columcille recognized his sin and repented and vowed to convert at least as many souls as were lost in the battle he instigated. Once he did that his reach grew much greater than it had been before. He began a ministry to the Picts through the conversion of their king. Columcille's new beginning in Iona has been long remembered and his legacy has been honored by modern day Christians on Iona. If he had not repented and instead held on to his anger and selfish

intentions, this would not have happened and who knows

how many more souls might have been lost.

> CHALLENGE: Is there unrepented sin in your life? Take a
> moment to contemplate this and repent. Even if you can't
> think of anything right now, ask God to forgive any misdeed
> you may have committed unknowingly.

> *Dear Father, forgive me. I want a new beginning because*
> *I know it is in these beginnings you do your best work.*
> *Set me on the right path and allow me a fresh start.*
> *Thank you for your mercy, which is never ending. Amen.*

BEGIN

Evening Forty

But when Sanballat, Tobiah, and Geshem the Arab heard of our plan, they scoffed contemptuously. "What are you doing? Are you rebelling against the king?" they asked. I replied, "The God of heaven will help us succeed. We, his servants, will start rebuilding this wall. But you have no share, legal right, or historic claim in Jerusalem."
Nehemiah 2:19-20 NLT

If you're looking for a story about beginning to rebuild, look no farther than Nehemiah. The walls of Jerusalem needed to be rebuilt. Nehemiah was just the man for the job. He organized, he influenced, he addressed scoffers, he prayed. He didn't sit around and complain. He got the job done, believing God would help him succeed and knowing that his mission from God gave his task credibility. The first step was to simply begin, to take action.

This story brings me back once again to St. Patrick. Even though there were Christians in Ireland before Patrick came to convert the island, Patrick was the most successful, he and those who followed his example even after he was gone. This conversion to Christianity came with almost no bloodshed unlike the later Eastern Mediterranean Crusades. Because the people believed the number three had magical powers, Patrick used the shamrock to explain that his God also had three natures. When they worshipped the lofty oak tree, Patrick introduced them to the One who created those trees. When the people esteemed the power of the moon, sun, and stars, when they marveled at the great power of the sea and the force of the wind, Patrick told them who held those powers that defined the forces of nature. Patrick and his followers took the beliefs the people already held, the power of the Creator they had already observed and honored, and by the authority God had granted him, much like Nehemiah, Patrick and his followers methodically built upon that foundation a new hope that endured.

> CHALLENGE: What will you begin to build today? God gives authority to those doing his work so make up your mind to begin!

> *Dear Father, I am grateful that you are the God of new beginnings. Even when I don't feel as though I have the strength to build new things, I know you do. Those you call, you equip. Thank you for this new beginning.*
> *Amen.*

CONCLUSION

This is not the end of your wanderings. You may want to wander through these pages again or begin a new devotional guide. You might need time to contemplate or to study scripture before beginning something new. The Christian life does not award degrees of achievement as if levels of understanding can be surmounted and then surpassed. We often have to circle around to an idea or precept we previously contemplated and that's all right. In fact, revisiting ideas can be positive and transformative. Embrace your wanderings and journey on!

[1] John J. O'Meara, translator, The Voyage of Saint Brendan, Journey to the Promised Land, (Gerrads Cross, Buckinghamshire: Colin Smythe Limited, 1976),10.

[2] Edward C. Sellner, *Wisdom of the Celtic Saints*, (Notre Dame, Indiana: Ave Maria Press, 1993), 23.

[3] Alexander Carmichael, *Carmina Gadelica: Hymns and Incantations with Illustrative Notes on Words, Rites, and Customs, Dying and Obsolete*. Edinburgh: Oliver and Boyd, 1928. Print.

[4] Esther de Waal, *The Celtic Vision*, (Liguori, Missouri: Liguori/Triump, 1988, 2001),88. Taken from the *Carmina Gadelica* III, 195.

[5] de Waal, *The Celtic Vision*, 164.

[6] A version of this poem can be found here: Whitley Stokes and John Strachan, editors, *Thesaurus Palaeohibernicus, vol. 2*, (Cambridge University Press, 1903), 290.

[7] John O'Donohue, *Anam Cara: A Book of Celtic Wisdom*, (New York: Cliff Street Books, Harper Collins, 1997), 14.

[8] Arna Roghnú AG and Pádraig O Fiannachta, *Saltair, Prayers from the Irish Tradition*, (Dublin: The Columba Press, 2000), 14.

[9] Cindy Thomson, *The Roots of Irish Wisdom: Learning From Ancient Voices*, (Independently Published, 2016), 81.

[10] Tracy Balzer, *Thin Places: An Evangelical Journey into Celtic Christianity*, (Abilene, Texas: Leafwood Publishers, 2007), 26.

[11] Esther De Waal, *Every Earthly Blessing: Rediscovering the Celtic Tradition*, (Harrisburg, PA: Morehouse Publishing, 1999), 86-87.

[12] Representative Body of the Church of Ireland, Holy Communion and Other Services of the Church of Ireland, (Dublin: Columba Press, 2013), 121.

[13] The rules of the ancient monks can be found in various places, including a translation by Uinseann Ó Maidín OCR, *The Celtic Monk, Rules and Writings of Early Irish Monks*, (Kalamazoo, MI: Cistercian Publications, 1996).

[14] https://www.irishtimes.com/opinion/remembering-the-sabbath-day-1.325313

[15] https://abbeyofthearts.com/blog/2020/04/04/monk-in-the-world-sabbath-6-questions-for-reflection-and-closing-blessing/

[16] Carmichael, *Carmina Gadelica: Hymns and Incantations with Illustrative Notes on Words, Rites, and Customs, Dying and Obsolete*

[17] The abbot Mochuda may not have been the author of the rule attributed to him. Some scholars believe the style is of later centuries so it may have been written by one of his successors.

[18] Some argue that round towers were not adequate defenses against raids because they could have been climbed or the monks could have been smoked out. Therefore,

they must have had another purpose. One could easily argue that they served as a lookout and deterred the raiders.

[19] Lady Gregory, *A Book of Saints and Wonders according to the Old Writings and the Memory of the People of Ireland*, (Dundrum, Ireland: The Dun Emer Press, 1906), book one, 6.

[20] Carmichael, *Carmina Gadelica: Hymns and Incantations with Illustrative Notes on Words, Rites, and Customs, Dying and Obsolete*

[21] Sellner, *Wisdom of the Celtic Saints*, 108.

[22] P.W. Joyce, *A Smaller Social History of Ancient Ireland*, (Dublin, Ireland: Longmans, Green, and Co., 1908, second edition), 372.

[23] Carmichael, *Carmina Gadelica: Hymns and Incantations with Illustrative Notes on Words, Rites, and Customs, Dying and Obsolete*

[24] Christine Valters Paintner, *The Soul's Slow Ripening, 12 Celtic Practices for Seeking the Sacred*, (Notre Dame, IN: Sorin Books, 2018), 39.

[25] Oliver Davies, *Celtic Spirituality*, (Mahwah, NJ: Paulist Press, 1999), 274.

[26] *The Glenstal Book of Prayer, A Benedictine Prayer Book*, (Dublin: The Columba Press, 2002), 113.

[27] Carmichael, *Carmina Gadelica: Hymns and Incantations with Illustrative Notes on Words, Rites, and Customs, Dying and Obsolete*

[28] Thomson, *The Roots of Irish Wisdom*, 37.

[29] University of Glasgow web site: https://www.universitystory.gla.ac.uk/biography/?id=WH1060&type=P

[30] Alfred Perceval Graves, *A Celtic Psaltery Being Mainly Renderings in English Verse from Irish & Welsh Poetry*, Public Domain.

[31] From *The Confession of St. Patrick*, which can be read here: https://www.confessio.ie

[32] Carmichael, *Carmina Gadelica: Hymns and Incantations with Illustrative Notes on Words, Rites, and Customs, Dying and Obsolete*

[33] Sellner, *Wisdom of the Celtic Saints*, 66.

[34] Gregory, *A Book of Saints and Wonders according to the Old Writings and the Memory of the People of Ireland*

[35] Sellner, *Wisdom of the Celtic Saints*, 145.

[36] Esther de Wall, The Celtic Way of Prayer: The Recovery of the Religious Imagination, (New York: Image Books, Doubleday, 1997), 119.

[37] Conrad Blady, *Brigid of the Gael: A Guide for the Study of St. Brigid of Kildare, A Source for Classroom Use*, (Linthicum, MD: Hutman Productions, 2000), 6.

[38] http://irisharchaeology.ie/2013/10/pangur-ban/

[39] J. Philip Newell, Sounds of the Eternal, A Celtic Psalter, Morning and Night Prayer, (Grand Rapids, MI: William B. Eerdmans Publishing Company, 2002), 44.

Made in the USA
Monee, IL
23 June 2023